Life Pig

PHOENIX POETS

ALAN SHAPIRO

Life Pig

THE UNIVERSITY OF CHICAGO PRESS

Chicago & London

ALAN SHAPIRO is the William R. Kenan Jr. Distinguished Professor of English at the University of North Carolina at Chapel Hill. A member of the American Academy of Arts and Sciences, he has published many books of poetry, including the National Book Award finalist *Night of the Republic* and the Pulitzer Prize finalist *Reel to Reel*; translations, *Trojan Women* and *The Oresteia*; two memoirs, *The Last Happy Occasion* and *Vigil*; and the novel *Broadway Baby*. A new book of essays, *That Self-Forgetful Perfectly Useless Concentration*, is also available from the University of Chicago Press.

The University of Chicago Press, Chicago 60637
The University of Chicago Press, Ltd., London
© 2016 by The University of Chicago
All rights reserved. Published 2016.
Printed in the United States of America

25 24 23 22 21 20 19 18 17 16   1 2 3 4 5

ISBN-13: 978-0-226-40417-2 (paper)
ISBN-13: 978-0-226-40420-2 (e-book)
DOI: 10.7208/chicago/9780226404202.001.0001

Library of Congress Cataloging-in-Publication Data
Names: Shapiro, Alan, 1952– author.
Title: Life pig / Alan Shapiro.
Other titles: Phoenix poets.
Description: Chicago ; London : University of Chicago Press, 2016. |
    ©2016 | Series: Phoenix poets | Includes bibliographical references.
Identifiers: LCCN 2016009808 | ISBN 9780226404172 (paperback :
    alkaline paper) | ISBN 9780226404202 (e-book)
Classification: LCC PS3569.H338 L54 2016 | DDC 811/.54—dc23 LC record
    available at http://lccn.loc.gov/2016009808

♾ This paper meets the requirements of ANSI/NISO Z39.48-1992
(Permanence of Paper).

To the memory of MARK STRAND *and* C.K. WILLIAMS

CONTENTS

ACKNOWLEDGMENTS

The author wishes to thank the following journals and magazines in which these poems or versions of them first appeared:

American Poets: "Vantage"
At Length: "Thanks for Nothing" (as "Gratitude for Nothing")
Cincinnati Review: "On the Beach" and "Goodness and Mercy"
Cortland Review: "Toward Language"
Johns Hopkins Review: "Low Tide" and "Dog Heart"
Mississippi Review: "Accident," "The Weeper," and "Dressing Table"
Plume: "Archimedes" and "Ghost of the Old Arcade"
Poetry: "Frieze"
Poetry Northwest: "Heavy Snow" (as "During Heavy Snow")
Warwick Review: "The Look"

LIFE PIG

The hams the hocks the oddly delicate
little busy trotters
dug in and pushing forward through the already grunted through
wet stink of what's been rooted up and chewed and
gobbled down to be shit
out in clumps and dribbles to be again ploughed
through like a harrow back
and forth across the pen for more and still more
scraps shreds fumes bacterial hints of fumes to feed on
so the hunger can keep feeding—
till at last the head lifts up
defiant nostrils pulsing wide
as if to suck in the even bigger pig of sun
which as it eats is glistening
inside the darkest beads and beadlets hanging from
the tip of every bristle on the snout.

One

THE HEBREW OUIJA BOARD

With yellowish dry skin, dark crooked teeth,
and her old-styled buttoned-up high-collared dress
with long sleeves covering her wrists, a dress
she almost seemed to hide in more than wear,
Mrs. Dubrow, a tiny woman, made herself
even tinier when she leaned down to watch us,
watch our faces take in the photograph,
our little bodies squirming in our seats—
her curly black hair jiggling angrily
as she nodded in approval without smiling,
walking from desk to desk in the picture's wake.
Look at it, she'd order us in a hoarse whisper,
you no better than a piece of wood
unless you look at it: a piece of wood.
White bodies, they were all piled up in stacks
beside a ditch, and the ditch was bible black,
a dirt absence blackening down as far
as the white bodies were neatly stacked up high—
like hay bales on top of hay bales made of breasts
crushed down on backs, on faces, legs between
legs opening or closing on a glimpse
of awful hair, of all the hidden parts
unhidden, but somehow made all right to look at
by being so meticulously bulked
and scrambled up together that any part
of one could have belonged to any other;

all sense of a real he or she with clothes on
buried, it seemed, by all the nakedness
around it, as if nakedness could be
something somebody else could do to you,
to hide you, cover you up with like a ditch
that made the ditch beside the bodies almost
beside the point. I couldn't look at them
or look away, I wanted to be nothing else
except the clothes I wore. I placed my hand
over them all and sat there till Mrs. Dubrow
put her dry hand on mine and moved it back
and forth and up and down so gently
she might have thought it was the scrambled up
alphabet of cheek, thigh, ankle, arm, or crotch
that moved the planchette of my hand across
the picture for the secret messages
the dead were passing back and forth from part
to hidden part about the bodies ours
would be, and what they'd touch and who would touch
them, where and how, inside some other picture
that her hand kept on deciphering through my hand.

THE HIAWATHA RECITATION

All along the schoolyard
blown out basement windows
of a warehouse
like a row of black mouths
seemed to suck our errant
kickballs past the white lines
of the game into the cellar
dark beyond our seeing,
lightless as the black pitch-water
stretching away inside the poem
we had spent the morning learning
to recite. Here we were crouching
on the lip of nothing looking
down into a dark so
damp with rot we
could have leaned against it,
leaning over some new unseen
dying there below us, like a
dare we couldn't stomach, peering
down at it, a solemn row of
little Hiawathas
all pretending any moment
any one of us might venture
to the bottom of the pit to
find the ball and bring it up out
of the mold of ages

back into the daylight,
savior of the lost game.
But as always when the bell rang,
we filed back into the classroom
to our row, our desk, our
primer opened to the same page—
where we now would read in
unison about the triumph and the
honor that for us existed
nowhere off the page, and even
on it now was crossed with
something shameful, something
unseen we could sense there
at the bottom of it,
always dying while along the
shore of Gitchee Gumee
of the shining Big-Sea-Water
all our voices went on
chanting out the
unrelenting march of
Hiawatha the avenger,
vanquisher of he who
sends the fever of the marshes
and the pestilential vapors,
and disease and death among us,
from the black pitch-water
and the white fog of the fen lands.

THE LOOK

I saw it without knowing
I had seen it
until I saw it again
years later in Plutarch's
Parallel Lives, the look
(I have to think)
not unassailable,
but not uncertain
either, and so, my father,
to discipline both
his urge to do and not
do what needed doing,
no matter how or
what he may have felt
about it, sought
asylum in the savage
un-anger of a look
of piety untempered
by anything but
piety, his face annealed
with it, as if the pain
he beat into the boy
my brother was—
because he what? had
shit himself? again?
or wet the bed?—was

not inflicted so
much by the father
that he was as by
the look or principle
the look upheld,
on which all hope
of being civilized
depends.
   As if he turned
just then into not
a father but a founding father
looking through the father
looking on as the sentence
in Plutarch's sentences
is carried out
right there before
the hushed assembly
upon the bodies of his two
sons, sons no longer,
but traitors now, mere
enemies of the tyrant-
hating new republic,
stripped by virtue, beaten
to death by piety, their then
beheaded heads staked
to the senate wall
as an example. The parallel
lives, the look, the
generation-stalking-
sacrificial-let-
this-be-a-lesson-to-you

look that is, as
Plutarch writes, so
god-like and so
brutish and thus so
very hard to praise
or blame too much.

TRAJAN'S COLUMN

Among the crammed-together tiny figures on a lower panel
of the frieze of figures coiling up the hundred-foot-high marble column

like a flowering vine of butchery and triumph, there's one figure
among the vanquished who, half naked, in profile slumps

against a wall—his face expressing nothing even while
he holds his arms out in hopeless supplication to the victor

towering over him with sword in mid-swing at its peak:
the killer's face too just as blank, mechanical, as if

it hardly had to do with him, whatever force it was
or law whose necessities he served, that played itself out

through this moment before it moved on to the next and the next
in a tumultuous unreadable sleepwalk through the hacking and

being hacked, spiraling up and away from us beyond what we can see.
The height of the column is the height of the great hill

the emperor razed to the ground, or his slaves did, shovelful by shovelful,
to build the tower to memorialize the glory, which the emperor himself was

really nothing but the humble servant of. Under the brick arch
of the concrete entranceway to the downtown factory where I worked

one summer there was this drunk, a woman, whose face, buried
in a mess of scarves, I never saw, whose body I had to step across

to get into the building, holding my breath against the almost solid
force field of stink around her, as if it were

my punishment for being not the one stepped over but
the one, head turned away, who got to do the stepping.

And I did it, and got used to it in no time really,
I admit it, my face blank, unreadable, and hard

as the concrete entranceway I entered by,
so that it came to seem simply the nature of the place,

an aspect of the job itself, the shrieking riveters and pressers I became
so good at running I could half doze as I stood there

hour after hour, day in day out, feeding them
the many different kinds of leather they obediently

would then shit out as many different kinds of belts
that women all over the city and the state would wear

while the belts were still in style, then donate to the poor when not.
Maybe, who knows, the drunk wore one of the belts we made.

But I didn't think about that then. Coming and going,
every moment of the day I didn't think of anything

till the summer ended and I returned to school,
as expected, then went beyond school, as expected too.

And not once did I ever think about that time and place, that woman;
not once till now, till my writing this about the lower panel

of a machine-like slaughtering that's only one of thousands
twisting up serenely to the very top of the column where

a statue of the good emperor used to stand, and now
a statue of St. Peter does, looking down triumphantly

on all that famous rubble at his feet.
The factory was shut down long ago.

And in its place colossal towers made entirely of glass rise up
so high that all you see now overhead are the rippling images

of buildings inside buildings, like a line of columns carved
from giant waves caught at the very moment they're about to break.

MOON LANDING, 1969

I don't remember now the names of anyone there,
or if I ever knew them, or even where there was,
maybe a friend's friend's apartment whose mother
if there was a mother might have been a single mom
who worked nights and wouldn't be around to hassle us.
What I remember mostly was the awful smell,
and the diffuse unease I moved in all that summer.
The lottery was coming soon; the lottery would surely
send me to the war I didn't think I'd have the guts to go to
or run from. All I wanted was to slow time down the way
a fast stream riffles over coarse grain, almost stopping
while it rushes forward never stopping, like me going party
to party to where what hadn't happened yet would never
happen even as it neared. The semicircle of the couch we
sat in, stupefied, facing the TV, was ripped and frayed, grayish
cotton batting under the weight of leg or arm
oozing out and then subsiding only to ooze out elsewhere
when any of us shifted, the carpet sticky, reeking of wet dog
crossed with cat piss though there was no cat or dog, the smell
unbearable until the smoke at last suppressed it,
until a cloud hung between us and the peace sign
of the antenna of the small TV whose screen carved from the dark
a little cave of gray-blue haze through which we watched
the seas of the moon rise slowly up to meet the lunar module
just as slowly coming down.

Then they were out in it,
first one and then another astronaut, clumsy in baggy white suits,
leap frogging like children underwater, little puffs of silt exploding
in slow motion at their feet. The flag flew straight out
as if made of hammered steel, stiff in a stiff wind, never rippling
or wrinkling, and lit up as by a spotlight someone said
must be the earth, and someone else said if it were the earth
then that must mean that from the moon the earth was the moon,
the moon's moon, someone else said, and we all laughed,
not knowing why.
            Then we fell silent as the astronauts stopped
goofing around, the sugar high of that first small step that
giant leap withdrawing till they looked like clowns
forlornly standing at mock attention in the tranquil sea
that wasn't tranquil or a sea, while the president thanked them,
promised to bring peace and tranquility to the very earth
that seemed just then to burn in the rigid flag, in the black glass
of the helmets, in the very specter of our own reflections
looking at ourselves look back across two hundred thousand
miles as the doobie like a shooting star inched over
the screen and through the Ort cloud of the swirling planetesimals
of our desolate tranquility breathing in and out.

GHOST OF THE OLD ARCADE

Under the giant chandeliers, in the sunless dazzle,
the objects of desire traded places with desire,

so that to stand there in the middle of that marble
avenue between the plate glass windows

of the shops was to be looked at by our own reflections,
looked at and imagined by them, as if our bodies,

the very matter of us, had been hallucinations all along,
airy specters of a gawking we had to see through

to see what it was we saw. We were always in the way
of what we wanted. Beyond the windows there were only

other windows, smaller windows, reflecting smaller versions
of our faces looking back at us as through the wrong

end of a telescope, adrift on glass vitrines, on the
jeweled surfaces inside them that we couldn't touch:

the diamond facets of a pin, or falling fixed
inside a frozen waterfall of rings and necklaces.

There was glassware too and cookware, glossy
leather bags and cases all backlit and glittering

as if forged of light by light that promised nothing
but perpetual brightening. And so

to pull away at last from the magnetic
weightlessness of all that showroom dreaming;

to tear ourselves from the untouched,
unsullied, the before we had it

having of it, was to trade reflection
for reflection, to see inside the giant prism

of that hall how with our bags and parcels
the body's shadow—shapeless as a sponge—

wiped clean all traces of us from the marble floor
that shone a little brighter for our having gone.

LET ME HEAR YOU

I am the disappearing point of an inverted pyramid
made from the two
before me, and the four before them
whom I know only as names
and snapshots, and farther back not even that, a
total namelessness fans out
without face or fact, no date,
no single anecdote or artifact,
barely a hundred years away
the family slate wiped back
into a clean abyss, a cenotaph
of lives only my body remembers
in ways I can't know about
even as I pass them
through me to my children
who through them will pass them on
to theirs, and theirs,
while I sink further down into no longer being known—

as if what even now I can't help think of
as the stately name-emblazoned
marble manor house of self
had all along been nothing but
a hut made not from mud or
even straw but
bits of ever-changing

string which
self is just the precious puppet of
no puppeteer is pulling,
blown about in planetary winds
no one can feel.

Outside is inside now.
The pyramid whose point
we are is weightless
and invisible
and has become itself the night
in which alone
together
on a high plateau
we go on shouting
out whatever name
those winds keep blowing back
into the mouth that's shouting it.

THANKS FOR NOTHING

Thank you, I don't know
who, or what,
for nothing
I can know
which something
once was spit from
for no reason
but to be
sucked back
to nothing so that
nothing could feel
what?—its nothingness
more keenly?

And thanks too for
the twin nothings
of past and future
that we imagine
coming from and
going to
within the un-
imaginable ever
suddenness of now
that passes by
so constantly it's like
it never passes,
which is how it passes.

And thank you for the accidental
wobble of the spinning
planet tilting back
from sun just far
enough to let
this fall day's chilly
burning away
of green before my eyes
go on burning
before my eyes
without my seeing.

And for these apples, too,
appearing only here
and there on the all
but hollowed-out
bent tree two fields away,
the biggest
of them bright as fire,
way too high to reach
while from the lowest branches
hang the smallest,
pocked, bruised, and so
misshapen you would
never guess how
white and crisp
the flesh is
underneath, or how
the juice spills
dribbling down the chin.

Thank you for my missing
wallet earlier today,
that instant of the worst
awakening when I was
reaching back
to the back
pocket, still safe
in my assumption
it was there,
still safely looking
out from within
the bubble of
everything I had
assumed so deeply
I couldn't see how
I'd been looking
through a blind
transparency
that's never noticed till
it's ripped away,
and suddenly I'm
falling in a clarifying
rush down through the
thought of just how
happy I had been
a moment earlier,
happy yet oh so
unaware inside
your heaven
of what hides
when I am in it

while it blinds me
with its brightness
when I'm not.

Thanks, truly,
for so little.
For the shifty,
ever-busy solace
behind the tortured
logic that would link
loss to beauty,
nectar to sorest need,
the clever ruses
we devise
to make of so little
given something
larger than it is.

And your quantum emissaries,
the blind, deaf, dumb
bacterial hordes
proliferating
through the cellular
abysses in the body
of the body that
the body on its own
without us as if
it weren't us fills
to empty, empties
to fill to turn the
hamster wheels

of need we run on
to outrun the need
that keeps us
just as tired
of running as we're
terrified to stop—
for that too
I should thank you.

But most of all
I give thanks
for the all
but unknowables of
whatever thirst
and hunger led me
in a sleepwalk
to this last, this
best love, never
stopping as I
faltered forward
till I found her.

Someday, not
today, not soon I hope,
I'll thank you
for the great blessing of
obliteration, yes,
even for that, especially
for that, the total
welcome of the total
dark where, if

I die before her,
I won't ever
have to know or see
whatever burden
my no longer being
there with her
might free her from,
what fresher pleasures
from whose newer touch
she'll seek—

And in the meantime
let me thank you
for last week
at the opening,
in the hall
with people milling
all around her,
cup of wine
in one hand, how she
somehow caught
my eye so I alone
would see her slyly
slip her free hand
down her pants
and out and
nonchalantly brush
her fingertips
across her nose
to breathe in
her own bouquet,

her pleasure
in herself so
nearly animal,
her pleasure
in my seeing it
so not; yes, thank you,
thank you so much for that.

And for the skin-
tight nearly see-
through lace chemise
that later in the half
dark seemed almost
made of mist,
the nearly nothing
of it that she had
to cross her arms
to take off
over her head
before she got
in bed beside me,

and the mischief
afterward, the sleights
of tongue and finger-
tip by which we
tricked each other
back to knowing
nothing of each other,
emptied of habit,
so intimately nothing

like ourselves
it was as if we'd
cheated on each other
with each other—
so when I picture it,
or try to now,
I can't imagine
who it is she is
imagining I am.

Which means, I think,
it's you I'm picturing,
you I'm longing for
and running from,
blind giver and dumb taker,
my stone deaf end
and origin, whom
I pretend
hears me pretend
to thank for being
both somehow
(I don't know how)
the dangled carrot
tempting me forward
into nothing and the stick
of nothing
nothing beats me with.

Two

VANTAGE

From where I watch, there are no highest leaves,
no leaves that don't have over them more leaves
impeding what they open up and out for,

darkening downward as they feed on green
diminishments, as if dark, if it still
can darken, could be itself the light

the darker leaves beneath are hungry for.
From where I watch even the shade hungers
and is hungered after—all along the chain

past bark, root, leaf, ghost speck of leaf,
microbial scrapings, and beyond them, flakes
chipped off of flakes off of a now-

no-longer anything, sucked dry, unsifted
and unsiftable into so fine a green
even the dark shines through. What's hunger but

a hole to fill, gravity of a self-
consuming, self-proliferating, blind,
and densely tangled maze of this from that,

from this, somewhere inside of which a cry
for mercy isn't heard, or is, and the jaws shut,
and the very dirt becomes the dirt of it.

THE KILLING

No sound more hellish
than the shrieking
from the woods last night
of something being killed—

the almost human screams
went on and on so far
beyond all hope of ever
stopping that when they

finally did stop, the after
echo lingered in the rustling
hush of what was eating it—
of what since it was eating

now was in no hurry,
and it was almost sexual—
the slowness of the sound
of gently being shaken,

the swish and whisper of the sheet-
like leaves, the bushes quivering
with the last quivers of
a hunger growing sweet

as heaven as it dies down.

LOW TIDE

On the mud flats
where I'm walking
each step pushes the wet
out from beneath it
to a dry halo

of a heel and toe
which as I lift it
dampens to
a trail of pools
behind me as I walk—

I make them all
along the flats and
when I circle back
they flash like lakes
seen from a plane

my body could be
the shadow of, inching
across the continent
down below, inside
of which invisibly

between the sand grains
in the infinitesimal

capillary spaces
closing and opening
under my steps are

creatures too small
to see or name
for whom each grain's
another land mass,
a different continent,

which makes the water
rushing in as my foot lifts
another ocean rushing out
as my foot falls,
so that wherever I go

quakes and floods,
subductions and extinctions
on a scale too
miniscule to register,
go with me—over

the mudflats happy
and thoughtless like
a leper without his bell,
wandering the world,
meaning no harm.

GREEN THOUGHT

There is a park nobody goes to now
where the leather swing seats of the swings hang slack
in a line of sad Us next to a castle of slides
and ramps, a parapet and staircase winding
around a tower so crooked you'd think it had
been frozen in the act of falling down.

A creek divides the park from a thin strip
of woods beyond it, a creek that's not a creek
but just a gully for runoff after rain,
a rocky, dry creek bed that's dotted here
and there with pools that after rain becomes
a sudsy rapids in the middle of which

the gnarled exposed roots of an old beech make
an islet of snakes for nesting condoms, needles,
flip-flops, and a brown bag full of empties.
By late fall past the leaf-clogged, shriveled creek
through bare trees there's a white apartment complex.
But in the spring, or summer after a rain,

if you should cross the footbridge over the creek
into the woods, the park and the apartments,
the swings and falling castle, and the complex
tall with the noise of living too far away
to hear, too everyday to bother hearing—
briefly and barely, all of it vanishes,

annihilated, you might even say,
to a green shade where, free of body, for
a moment overhead, you can almost see it,
the marvel of a willing nectarine
and peach bending the end branches to the hands
that only have to open, never reach.

TOWARD LANGUAGE

Invisible inn we live inside,
that lives inside us, that not one of us
remembers ever entering, or knows
most of the time inside it that
we're even there inside it, talking
in sleep to one another as
we sleepwalk down the corridors
we dream our passing through
will brighten and warm.
                              Anthill of sound,
the most accomplished of its drones
up the ever-steepening slope
of it will spend a lifetime pushing
a tiny grain another drone
pushing another grain even tinier
will bury.
                Airy burial mound
out of a happenstance of mouths
it uses to confect its own emergence—
even the most intimate
articulation summoned up
inside us isn't ours, and isn't
intimate, and yet without it
is there an ours at all?
                        Is this what freedom is
inside this prison house, your hand
pressed up against the glass

my hand is pressing as we face
each other, each other's visitor
and inmate, as the hour grows late?
Tell me, before you go, or I do,
just what it is you see through this
transparent blindfold, this dividing
revealing mistrusted and yearned for
what next what now what not of
tell me and I'll tell you.

STELE
Third Century BCE Greek

The mother's face in profile—
looking toward foreign sunlight
pouring in through the window—
is looking from the upper fragment,
which is rounded at the top
and crumbled inward
toward the bottom
where her neck and shoulder
ought to be, where only wall is now.
The bottom of it balances,
or seems to, on the fragment under it
of a robed breast, under which
on the mother's lap the arm
descending from the missing
shoulder surrounds a baby
squirming to look up and back
at something over the shoulder
that isn't there.
        The mother's face
is stately, composed, almost absurd
in its dignified stiff refusal
to acknowledge that her robe's
been pulled back and bunched
up high on her thigh
by all the baby's squirming
to see whatever it is

behind the mother
that in the stopped
instant of the scene
somebody else, the husband
maybe, had wanted put there
to remind himself
until he joined them in the tomb
of just how curious
in life the baby was,
how patient the mother.

It is as if the mother thinks
that time has stopped for the two of them,
or would stop if only
the foreign sunlight
wasn't inching every moment
closer to illuminate
a restlessness and patience
long since out of date.
If only it wasn't seeping
up her thigh now, over
the bunched robe and squirming baby,
brightening on the wall
a moment where the neck and shoulder
should have been before
it rises to the face,
which almost seems to
harden against its own
illumination, so as to preserve
the pretense that it isn't
centuries away and doesn't

know she's just a figure
on a tomb that's crumbled out
from under her to these
broken pieces of a raft
they drift apart on without moving,
she and the baby, lost
as the sunlight of a day
two thousand years ago
this sunlight imitates,
pouring in and washing
over and carrying away
with subatomic patience
both the patient mother
and the restless child who
in her very stillness
won't sit still, twisting
and squirming to
glimpse behind the mother
whatever it was in life
she couldn't wait to see.

FRIEZE

Over an edge of cloud the naked angel
blasts his long horn downward and they rise,
or try to, skeletons, half skeletons,
the still fleshed bodies of the newly dead,
rising and pushing up the stone lids, heaving
the crypt doors open, clambering over one
another, dumbstruck, frightened, warily peeking
out from inside tombs, or out of ditches,
their eyeholes blacker than the black they peek from
while some reach out of habit for a robe
to hide a nakedness they have no longer,
a phantom shame that must be all the bones
remember of the living flesh they were,

and all of them worn away to nearly nothing,
more wisp of form than form, more wraith than wisp,
as if before your eyes they're sinking into
what they're rising out of, coming into view
by fading from it, there and gone, as if
the very stone, unsure of what it holds,
can neither cling to nor relinquish now
the dream of something in it more than stone,
other than hard or heavy, as over the face
of it the air of a wished-for morning ripples
the robes to water while it washes through
the skulls and half skulls tilted back to see
just what the noise is that won't let them sleep.

DOG HEART

How he can't not be
where I am, how
his head lifts if I
so much as shift
in my chair, or sigh,
or how he, when I
stand, stands
to follow me from
room to room, to
kitchen to yard to
back inside to again
flop at my feet
and sleep, or seem to,
one ear cocked and
half turned, ever
listening for the slightest
gesture of the pre-
hint of a sign of
being left behind,
and why and for
how long—oh
the claustral weight
of his needing what
he can't have but for me

recalls the dog heart
of an old love,
loved and hated,
hated for being loved,
the heavy scentless
feedback loop
of that devotion fed
by her aversion
fed by that devotion's
dog heart way
too avid to please her
to ever please her,
that even now
so many decades
later can find
itself sometimes
(not often) there
at the door she closed
for good behind her,
staring at it, staying
just as he was told
to stay, the way
he never could
back then, right there,
good boy, good boy,
where he was left.

SCAT

Her voice the voice of hunger
when from another room

she's singing, unaware
of me, or just not caring

that I hear her, hear
that hunger no one song

can sate as restlessly
she wails, she croons,

she rhapsodizes be bop
into do wop into

torch song, ditty, dirge
in a continuous feed-

back loop of words wet
with their own emergence

out of sound dissolving
back to sound emerging

like a vocal time lapse
running up and down

her voice and through it
hungrily past self

past specie even and
beyond through every long

dead sediment and overlay
of its becoming—down

to the underwater
burning at the bottom of it all

on the lip of which
up through the vent of

voice still audible
even now that

Ur scat of a first
cell howling to be fed.

ON THE GREENWAY BEHIND MY OLD HOUSE

If who I was twenty years ago had seen us out back
behind his house beyond the fence on the other side of the brook
looking in through the understory as he slammed the screen
door and paced the yard, kept pacing as he often did
in those days, playing back whatever angry scene
had driven him from the house for safety's sake because
who knows what he might have done to her or himself
or God forbid the children, what he was capable of
doing or destroying inside the shrinking cage
of that moment of a rage increasing with every step he took;

if he could have seen me, ghost from an unimaginable future,
out there with you, his next wife, who back in those days
would have been the very image of a life he'd been
deprived of, certain he always would be, having grown by then
clairvoyant with all he didn't have—if he had seen us there
beyond the fence over twenty years away on a fall day
in a shower of green-gold leaves flashing in brighter sun
and blacker shadow—he would have turned away in disbelief.
He would have gone back inside, slamming the door
against this haunting from a life he couldn't help

but think of as a dream dreamed by the hopped up pain
no pain could satisfy, no misery ever misery enough.
And as we stood there I could almost hear him asking,
"What are you doing here, why come back at all

except to see how happiness might be, for you,
just another way to suffer, trickier, never to be trusted,
making that past life almost something to be missed
if only because it's out of reach across the brook
beyond the understory on that side of the fence
where you don't have to go now even if you could?"

IN THE HOTEL ROOM

of the forbidden history
of my affection,
the TV screen on or off
stays blank as Buddha's mind,
forever channel surfing
to itself inside itself through reruns
of what no one else will ever see.
Room service is always calling me
for room service
for whatever I am out of.
The privacy please
placard hangs from the inside latch
of the bolted door
to remind me of the room
without me in it,
so that in it I am elsewhere,
in another room identical to this,
imagining other men before me
on the bed with you, whoever you were then,
doing what they did
with someone other than
the woman they believed you were.
Two sealed bottles of expensive water
aloof and haughty stand side by side
on the minibar beside the bed
and in the giant mirror behind the bed

two other bottles watch them
in amused transparencies of thirst.
And on the bed itself, on the bed
I so want to lie down in
and never do
so I'll always want to—sits
a suitcase in my place,
a suitcase that depending on the mood
has either just been packed
or opened so that either way
for whomever's next to me
I'll be always just arriving
or departing,
which is how I stay.

PRESENT

I'm sitting on the bed where I've been told to sit,
watching her at the full-length mirror shimmy
out of jeans and jersey and then slip on the new dress
she tells me five months before her birthday is
the birthday present I am giving her. What do I think?

She tugs the hem down and wiggles slightly as she slides
one hand then the other over the in-curve of waist
and out of hip, half turning side to side while leaning back
as if to gauge the quality, the exact degree of
pleasure she would feel if she were someone else

like me, for instance, or a younger version of me, taller,
no longer balding, seeing herself pass by. So? She asks again,
her eyes now in the mirror locked on my eyes locked on her hand
as it leads my seeing down over hip to thigh and then back up again—
What do I think? I think my taste is pretty good, to which

she says, I don't look fat? And I say after a moment, well
maybe, just a little—because I know at that she'll whirl round,
arms akimbo, the fabric tighter as her chest swells, nipples erect
with outrage—the flush of anger in her cheek now almost like
a blushing girl's, a girl pretending she's a woman

wagging a finger at the boy I almost think, just then,
I am.—And isn't this, Time, how we think to fool you,
even now, late as it is, like children home alone
in a shadow play of giving to each other
the very gifts you're every moment taking back?

Three

ON THE BEACH

Inside the nineteen fifties of my sexual sleep and terror,
in the middle of a beach of bodies on display for purposes
I even then could tell were all the more impersonal
for seeming not to be, in different phases of undress,
among transistor-distant wreckages of songs and insect
buzz of voices breaking in with news as the surf boomed
as it broke, then hissed withdrawing under a sky so
lavishly blue so endless in its blueness even I knew
it had to be the sky of only there and only then,

all afternoon, I dug a little hole. I scooped up white sand
out of white sand, beside my mother's animal grunts and ohs,
laughter, far off screams, boom and hissing as my father
spread white cream across her, rubbed the cream to oil,
the oil to sheen, all over arms and belly up and down
each leg and furtively on the inside of her thighs
up even to the little curly hairs I didn't know just how I knew
I shouldn't have looked at while I looked at them, kept
looking at them in the moments no one saw me looking.

My hand the shovel, my fingers the mechanical claw,
I dug out a shelter for myself like the one my father said
we didn't have the money for, like the one the radio
assured us would keep us safe as money in a safe, a pile
of gold coins in a bank vault never to be spent, and anyway,
on what, for what, what kind of life would that be,

he was asking with his eyes closed in the only there and then
of hands that slid in circles over the ohing body,
while the hot sand grew cooler the further down I dug,

cooler, dark, and damp, and when I pulled my hand back,
water seeped up between the grains and when I paused
would instantly subside into what would instantly
grow paler and dryer; damp then dry, dark then pale, then dark
under the sky no bomb would fall from, not today, not here,
even though her body glistened, all of her wet with beads of light
except the little hairs high up on the inside of the thighs,
as if all but that of her, forbidden and unignitable,
had vaporized before my eyes under his furtive hands.

HER CLOSET

What little air there was inside it was so completely black
and thick it could have almost been itself a fabric,
a black barely breathable woven emanation

from the clothes jammed together on the rack
I'd slip through, to where I didn't have to close my eyes
to close my eyes, so deep inside it I was of it

more than in it, I was the feeling thread of her having gone:
I was how the clothes she didn't wear that day
could breathe in ghostly frays of perfume and remember,

mourning, how they hung deflated, shapeless, colorless,
in the black sky that they themselves composed
of her not being there, as if the farthest away

of anything there was or ever could be was
all along right there inside the closet where I went
to find the endlessly absent body brought so near.

DRESSING TABLE

The little pot of shadow for the eyes, and the fine tip
of the brush hairs she called a pencil she would dip
into the pot and brush along the lashes, lash to lash,

blue jar of cream so white it was a mystery
it wasn't food though it was like her skin would eat it
when it went across first one cheek then the other

from white to moist, to beige case that held beige pad
and powder, red case that held the rouge, and the gold
vial of perfume that even screwed on tight effused

unbreathable sweetness all around itself
among the many different colored tubes
of lipstick she would, depending on the mood,

open and twist up into an orange, pink, or reddish tip
sloped inward toward her by its having
rubbed so many times across her pursed lips.

But scariest of all was the silver jewelry box
she'd sift through in the final stage of being ready,
the glitter and clink of necklaces and bracelets

spilled out like fish scales scraped and shredded,
and the sprawl of rings and earrings, pins and broaches
urgently going in or out, or on or off while she

would watch herself both queen and subject,
abject and haughty, as desperate to please as she was
unappeasable, staring not at but into what was staring back

from deep inside the mirror, inside whose brass rim
was a lamp that lit the glass that magnified the face
that looked back up at her while she looked down at it,

both warped as in a fun house where there was no fun
besides this face, this slow, painstaking, merciless,
submissive face—traceless and smooth as every nail

after paint and polish, and the emery board
is back in its stiff packet neatly stacked on top
of others out of sight in a corner of the drawer.

THE BEDROOM

As if to scold it for having had the nerve to kink and wrinkle,
she'd give the top sheet one sharp tug and then another,
and then stretch it out so tightly you'd think that nothing
could ever wrinkle it again. And once the pillows had been
plumped to showroom fullness, she'd flap the coverlet three times,
each time a little higher, till almost by its self it billowed down
obediently over the bed, after which, with her hand held sideways
like a blade, she'd cut a straight line in the coverlet
from her side to his along the bottom of the pillows.

Everything held its breath. Even the smallest dust mote
hung in the air, invisible, afraid to fall. Even the finest hairs
of pile in the shag carpet crushed from the vacuum cleaner
were afraid to unbend, lift up, be seen and driven down again.
Everything played its part in the hallucination
as long as possible to make the room an empty scene
on a stage inside a theater in which all seats were reserved seats
with nobody ever in them, and there was never any way
to tell if the play had ended or hadn't yet begun,

except for what lay under the glass lampshade in the lamp light
on the bedside table—the pack of Marlboro's
with its barely wrinkled cellophane aglitter beside a beveled
ashtray with a cigarette, half smoked, unstubbed,
leaning on its lip, a smudge of lipstick like red dirt

all around the filter while the tip still smoldering sent up
a thin thread of a signal that slowly twisted till it split
in two, and the two split thinning into two more into the nearly
nothing of a signal nobody there would ever dare decode.

THE PIG

The 1950s of her dream persisted
Into the 1960s,
Confident at first,

Despite the first awakenings around it,
Even a little smug,
Unthreatened, but then as more and more awoke

It grew confused, mystified, furious,
Retreating to a last redoubt—
Part farce,

Part suicide mission—
Of her wanting us
Never to help her with what she did alone

While wanting every one of us
To see her do it every evening
As her fork scraped uneaten scraps

Down the hole of the disposal
That she called the pig
And flipped the switch

To hear it churn
All she'd done for us
To nothing,

The dishes scoured and sparkling on the rack,
The table scrubbed to chilly radiance,
The floor swept,

She never wanting us, not once, not
Ever, to help her do it,
Not even on the nights she herself refused to do it,

Had had enough
Already and would sit there
At the bomb site of the table,

Cigarette burning down between her fingers,
Untouched cup of coffee steaming
Till it didn't,

She wanting us to see her stare at nothing, see
Her not care if we saw
How she had gone away

Like food scraps down the pig
Of nowhere we could follow
Where the dream churned

On itself down through the void
Of its persistence
Among the wreckage all the waking up had wrought.

HEAVY SNOW

When she tells me how they used to go out walking
in heavy snow, at night, and the snow would turn
the city to a stage set of a city, and how to be out walking in it
was to walk inside a play about two people walking
arm in arm down the middle of avenues great drifts
on either side had reimagined into lanes, lanes into alleyways,
no tracks, no prints but theirs, and theirs filled
to effacement almost as soon as made, so every step
became its own path leading only to wherever it was
they went for the one and only time they went there;

when she describes cars buried to the very tips of their antennas,
steam from lips obscuring now and then a face
they might have come upon, companionably greeting
one another as they at any other time would never do,
street signs unreadable, storefronts frosted over, nameless,
I picture it all as she describes it, except in my imagining
I never let them turn around. I keep them walking
out across unbroken snow farther away with every step
from every step that would have led them back to the empty
house's separate bedrooms where antipodes of bedsheets

chilled under snow-white counterpanes flat as ice.

GOODNESS AND MERCY

I bolted upright
at the panting
O Ga O Ga O Ga
where she too weak too
breathless to lie down
or lie back just shook
her head at my What Ma

What do you need morphine
the nebulizer What
can I do for you to which
the inwardly collapsing
gummy horizontal
wrinkle of a mouth
pushed out another O Ga

while I couldn't not
look down at the nightgown
hanging off one shoulder
below a shriveled
dug it was my grief
to see her grief
to see me see it

her grief and maybe
outrage maybe payback
too for that
and for her hearing
in my exhausted
You okay now
a half suppressed

impatient What
What is it this time
Even goodness
did no good was
merely dutiful
O Ga O Ga
Thou shalt not see

the shriveled dug
I saw or hear
the toothless cries
for help that were refusing
help to make the cries
more righteous
the help less kind

O Ga that's how the night
passed and the next
night and the next and how
we each endured it
each in our own way I
the ancient infant's
babbled plea or curse

and she the put-upon
mere goodness
that wanted it over with
yet never failed
to bolt up when she cried
and find her there like that
the way he did.

SWEETNESS AND NIGHT

Long past indignant at the loss
of dignity, almost amused
by it, but not, every moment

of the day a strip search in public,
every breath a punishment
for what? she couldn't say,

which makes her no less
penitent, sitting forward,
head bowed, in the chair

she can't get out of
without help, which is itself
another punishment,

or would be if she weren't
past it now, almost amused
but not, staring at the floor,

having to keep staring at it
before she'll let you
help her up

as if to stare it into place,
as if to keep it under her,
as if to make sure before

she stands it isn't being
dreamed to trick her
into standing up

on nothing—
so it can see her fall,
whoever or whatever it is

that's doing this to her,
that's getting her,
or would be,

if she weren't past
being gotten to, almost
amused, but not,

almost not caring
if she doesn't make it
in time across the room

to the toilet because
the ruin is total,
or nearly so.

What's left to feel
to feel how
funny, how

free of it she is.

ACCIDENT

Before the wreckage of waking
again in a wet bed,
in the not yet awakened
pre-moment of it dawning on her,
when the pressure easing is
as much a promise as
a feeling, the release
so new that even
as it starts to happen
is still about to happen,
the warmth between the legs
just warmth, not wetness yet,
the sheets still dry—

in those vanishing last seconds
of not knowing, on that
disintegrating raft,
that shrinking margin of a
warmth not wet yet,
the wet not cold, before
the cold rash of waking,
who's to say before she wakes
she isn't still a child,
a baby, who, because
she's just a baby,
is waking up to only
pleasure in a blameless bed?

MOTHER PALINODE

What if it wasn't morphine only
that caused the startling
late turn into what
did really seem
more
like kindness than the niggling almost
angry tit-for-tat performances
of being kind?

What if it wasn't only Percocet
that toward the end had
loosened the life-
long clung-to
grip
of injuries too deep to be
ever quite forgotten
or recalled—

that opened wide the pinched
compass of concern
beyond the why
me of so much
pain
expanding up to and beyond
the outer reaches of the
endless universe

inside the shrunken body—
And if it wasn't that,
what was it?
What do I
make
of, do I do with, each time
I leave her, how
she lifts

a curled hand trembling to her lips
to kiss the fingertips which
open slowly and
unevenly
till
she can, who can hardly
see or breathe now,
purse her lips

and blow in no particular
direction as if it
didn't matter
what or
who
that purely grateful,
already ghostly
kiss was for?

THE WEEPER

Except for the last days,
her lips at the phantom-faint
first quiver of feeling
would tighten to stuff it back
down into whatever hidey hole
of shame the feeling hid in
when it wasn't trying to be felt,

as if the worst nightmare
imaginable would have been
that face, that fixed
expression collapsing into
sideshow freaks
of expression so extreme
they're almost sexual,

a kind of sex with strangers
in front of strangers, the
stripped bare grotesqueries
of complete release
on a gurney in the fluorescent clinic
of complete humiliation.
Except for the last days.

In the last days all she did
no matter who was there
was weep, weep
silently, suddenly,
at any moment
while her hands rose
to her face, though not to hide it—

no, but just to touch it
lightly, the way the blind do,
this thing she could no longer
keep herself from doing,
this almost language foreign
to her fingers that her fingers
had to feel to read.

THE LAST OUTING

Before you'd let me "take you for a quick spin" around the building
in your wheelchair because the evening was unseasonably warm
and still light and who knew when you'd feel this well again—
you had to "put your face on"—eyeliner, rouge, lipstick, pink
matching the blanket on your knees, sparse hair brushed,
a dab of perfume on each palm and on the neck to mask the smell
that only you and I could smell since no one else was out there,
just you, just me behind you pushing the chair slowly as I could
over cracked asphalt to the back of the building where the pool was,
empty and dry, dead leaves lining the bottom, plastic lounge chairs
stacked up under awnings, and on either side of us bushes,
leafless and dense, were quivering with birds it was by then too dark to see,
twigs shaking and going still before now here now there they shook again
and all so silently—no wing whir or muffled cheeping—it was as if
the barren wicker work was shaking from itself lost memories of birds,
their urgent absences.
                    A siren on the far edge of hearing, so faint
it was more rumor of a sound than sound, broke open the silence,
and suddenly in rushed a rage of traffic, horn blare and screech of brakes,
and somewhere from an upper window back behind us
a hoarse voice, sexless and old, scolded a pet or spouse,
Now look what you've done! Look at it!
And as if too suddenly awakened, you straightened up and
heroically it almost seemed pulled out from under the blanket
a silver compact and held its little mirror up before your face

to check your lipstick, tuck in a few stray hairs, fuss with the hairdo
till it was just so, so when I'd wheel you back around the building
through the lobby to your shrinking room you'd look presentable,
just like yourself again, in case anyone were there.

ARCHIMEDES

Bent over the plate, she studies
the tremor in the hand that
holds the fork that
lifts the food that
when it's lifted, trembling,
spills back to the plate.

Head down, puzzling it out,
she doesn't see
and while she doesn't
maybe isn't there
in the lunchroom hearing
the linoleum echo
of the half words and
disconnected phrases
others at the table
say to no one
in response to nothing.

She could be pondering how wide
the gulf is between
tine and tongue, and cup and lip,
or why it is the hand won't
hear her, won't listen, is it
deaf, or stubborn,
a stubborn brat holding its breath

and shaking till it gets its way
though it won't tell her
what its way is,
what it wants from her.

And as she stares it down
as if by staring she might
shame it into being hers again,
or untangle the knotted
up enigma
of how the present had been
always only present
even while it carried her
from house to cottage to
apartment to
this linoleum-echo
of disconnection
in a lunchroom
of strangers in a home
that isn't
with a hand that won't
stop shaking from the fork
whatever food is
being lifted to her mouth.

THE SIBYL'S NURSING HOME

Her room is a stone cube of darkness
the lit screen of the TV
can't push off of itself,
a mineral heaviness
nearly smothering
the audience's almost dumb show
shrieking that is mite-size,
far away as from another room,
or planet, while the Old Sibyl
shrinks through the centuries
of the afternoon in her recliner,
head slumped to chest,
remote pressing hand
to armrest, holding it there
to hold her there where
nothing but sunlight
happens through the bent slats
of the shut blinds
cracking the dark in two
across her chin
in a mute slow
lightning flash
which thins as it rises
from bottom lip to upper
lip to eyes to nothing
but dark again before it flashes

again tomorrow at the same time
across her ever shrinking
into never being
gone beyond the almost
inaudible tiny
shrieking of the screen.

TERMINAL RESTLESSNESS

Sensation of shifting
absences, of hide-
and-seek under bright
fluorescence just
beyond her seeing
but so close to being
seen that being seen
is like a promise
her long dead children
can't keep but
can't stop promising—
peripheral vapor trails
her turning to
disperses—her turning from
draws back—draws
back from out to just
out of the reach of
now behind her now
before her there on this
side when she turns
to that—cruel play-
mates of a final
Ollie ollie oxen free
of the body by
the body to
the body till
the seeking stops.

ENOUGH

That prayer to you
to let her please God
die already, prayed
daily in the presence
of the ones who loved her
so as to punish
the ones who loved her
for not loving her
enough—that prayer must
surely have amused you,
Lord, as it didn't them—
why else not grant it
all those years as one
by one they all
died off till only one
was left, the one who,
though he never prays,
is praying now
to tell you knock it off,
you sick fuck, this isn't
funny anymore,
every breath now
just a plea for breath
you give her just enough
of so the breathlessness
keeps breathing—what's
the point? She's done

with us, but you, you
endless fooler, inexhaustible,
insatiable, whom I
don't even think
exists, you're never done
with us, or her, not
even now when there is
hardly anybody there
to get the joke.

VISITATION

When I put the fork down
too close to the edge of the table
no one was saying,
Put it on your plate for God's sake
before you knock it over!
No one kept her lonely watch
against the filthy, shameless,
ever-advancing
drift and accident the kitchen was
whenever she wasn't
in it scrubbing away
the constant onslaught of it all.
The fork lay dangerously near the edge.
Crumbs had fallen from it
too small to see
or sweep away while
overhead across the light, her long watch over,
inside dust column
after column
she as dust was falling
onto all the helpless surfaces
she wasn't there to clean.

Coda

DEATH HOG

Maw of the breeding mud
     of the barnyard of the planet
          in a paradise of being fed

by bodies gobbling
     bodies while it wallows
          at the bottom of it all,

at all times belly up—
     deaf, dumb, and blind,
          a sinkhole

of a massive infinitesimal
     infant-sucking
          growing emptier

the more it fills, the more
     we fill it, squawking
          scratching pecking

at the dirt we sink into
     for any morsel of why,
          any gorgeous hogwash

of a crumb to prettify
     or hide or just prolong
          the sinking—too hungry

to find it, or to see how,
      when we do
            find it, swallowing

whole some notion
      that it's the lion's
            claw and tiger's tooth

that have given
      the deer its grace
            and beauty and speed,

we sink the same, even
      as we swallow.
            Even then it feeds.

NOTES

"Thanks for Nothing" is dedicated to Ross Gay, inspired by his "Catalog of Unabashed Gratitude."

In "Low Tide," the closing image derives from Graham Greene's *The Quiet American* (1955).

"Toward Language" is dedicated to Charlie Baxter.

In "Death Hog," the sentence "it's the lion's claw and tiger's tooth that have given the deer its grace and beauty and speed" is from Edward Abbey's *Desert Solitaire* (1968).